The Science of Living Things

HOW DO ANIMALS FIND FOOD?

Bobbie Kalman

Crabtree Publishing Company

www.crabtreebooks.com

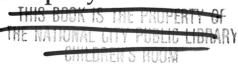

The Science of Living Things Series
A Bobbie Kalman Book

For my adorable baby grandson
Sean Lorne

Author and Editor-in-Chief
Bobbie Kalman

Research
Kathryn Smithyman
Heather Levigne

Editors
Heather Levigne
Kathryn Smithyman
John Crossingham
Amanda Bishop

Computer design
Kymberley McKee Murphy

Production coordinator
Heather Fitzpatrick

Consultant
Patricia Loesche, Ph.D., Animal Behavior
Program, Department of Psychology,
University of Washington

Photographs
Joe McDonald Wildlife Photography: Joe McDonald: page 18
Photo Researchers Inc.: Tom McHugh: page 15
Roger Rageot, David Liebman: page 19
Tom Stack & Associates: Jeff Foott: page 28; Thomas Kitchin:
    page 1; Kitchin and Hurst: page 20; Joe McDonald:
    pages 21, 25 (bottom); Dave Watts: page 29
Other images by Adobe Image Library and Digital Stock

Illustrations
Barbara Bedell: pages 5 (middle), 6 (bottom middle),
    19 (top right and bottom), 26 (middle left), 31
Cori Marvin: page 17 (right)
Jeanette McNaughton-Julich: page 28
Margaret Amy Reiach: page 24 (top right and left)
Bonna Rouse: pages 5 (bottom), 6 (bottom right and left),
    7, 8, 9, 12, 15, 17 (left), 19 (top left), 24 (bottom),
    26 (bottom right and left), 29

Separations and film
Embassy Graphics

Printer
Worzalla Publishing

Crabtree Publishing Company
www.crabtreebooks.com   1-800-387-7650

PMB16A
350 Fifth Avenue
Suite 3308
New York, NY
10118

612 Welland Avenue
St. Catharines
Ontario
Canada
L2M 5V6

73 Lime Walk
Headington
Oxford
OX3 7AD
United Kingdom

Cataloging in Publication Data
Kalman, Bobbie
    How do animals find food?
        p. cm. -- (The Science of living things)
        Includes index.
    ISBN 0-86505-986-1 (library bound) ISBN 0-86505-963-2 (pbk.)
    This book introduces children to carnivores, herbivores, cooperative
hunters, and other animals that find food in fascinating ways.
    1. Animals—Food—Juvenile literature. [1. Animals—Food habits.]
I. Title. II. Series: Kalman, Bobbie. Science of living things.
QL756.5.K35 2001
591.5'3—dc21

LC00-069367
CIP

Contents

Why do animals eat?

Animals are living things. All living things need **energy** to survive. Food provides the energy animals need to grow, move, make homes, have babies, and defend themselves.

The type of food an animal eats depends on where it lives. To get food, animals may hunt in grasslands, dive deep in oceans, or catch food in midair.

How animals find food also depends on how their body is built. An animal's body is **adapted**, or suited to, the type of food it eats. As time passes, groups of animals develop physical features, such as strong jaws or long legs, which make it easier for them to find and catch food.

Some birds have longer legs and beaks than others. Long legs and a long beak enable this bird to reach food under water without getting its body wet.

Different diets, different names

Animals that eat plants, fruits, seeds, or flower **nectar** are called **herbivores**. **Carnivores** are animals that eat other animals. If an animal eats both plants and animals, it is called an **omnivore**. Animals that eat mainly insects are called **insectivores**. Many animals are **opportunistic feeders**—they eat whatever they can find. **Scavengers** feed on dead animals killed by carnivores. **Decomposers** eat leftover bits of dead plants and animals. They play an important role in keeping the earth clean.

Rhinoceroses are herbivores that eat grass.

Bears eat plants, fish, or whatever food they find.

Food chains

All energy comes from the sun. Plants use the sun's energy to make food. When an herbivore eats a plant, the energy from the sun passes into the animal's body. When a carnivore eats an herbivore, the energy then passes into the carnivore's body. This pattern of eating and being eaten is called a **food chain**. The areas in which animals live, called **ecosystems**, differ in their soil, climate, or plant life. There are unique food chains in each ecosystem. In forests, mice eat berries, and then eagles eat the mice. On African savannas, zebras eat grass, lions eat zebras, and vultures clean up the leftovers.

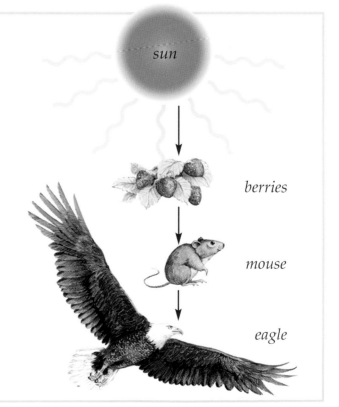

sun

berries

mouse

eagle

How do animals find food?

Animals come in many sizes, shapes, and colors. Some have hard skeletons on the outside of their body. Others have a skeleton that is held up by a **spinal column**, or backbone. Insects, worms, jellyfish, sharks, whales, birds, snakes, crabs, frogs, and monkeys are all animals. Their bodies differ, and so do their methods of finding food. They rely on their senses to locate food and then use their own specialized methods of getting it.

Waiting for food to come

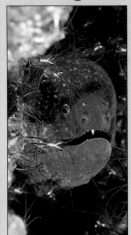

Many animals wait for food to come to them. They set traps for their prey or hide among plants or rocks. This moray eel is hiding in a coral reef.

Camouflage

Markings or colors that help an animal blend in with its surroundings are called **camouflage**. Chameleons can change their body color to match leaves or rocks. They then sit still and wait for prey.

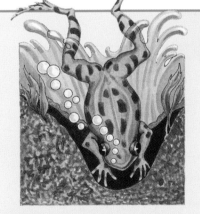

Hibernation

Food is difficult to find during cold winters. Some animals, such as frogs and ground squirrels, **hibernate**, or sleep until spring. During this deep sleep, the animal uses the food energy that is stored in its body fat.

Making food

Sometimes the best way to get food is to make it yourself! Honeybees make food using the nectar they gather from flowers. They store the honey in wax honeycombs so they will have enough to eat during the winter.

Migration

Many animals, such as birds and whales, **migrate**, or travel long distances each year, to find food. The tern lives in the Arctic in summer but hunts in South America in winter.

Using lures

Some predators are too slow to chase prey, so they lure their prey toward them. The anglerfish has a growth on its head that looks like a morsel of food. When a curious fish gets close, the anglerfish lures it into its mouth.

Poison

Some animals use poison to **paralyze** their prey. **Venomous** snakes have sharp, hollow fangs. When they bite an animal, poison flows through the fangs and into the animal.

Grazing and browsing

Grazing animals eat mainly grass. **Browsers** eat leaves and other parts of trees. Giraffes are browsers. Their long neck allows them to eat the leaves of tall trees that other animals cannot reach.

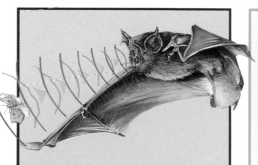

Echolocation

Bats and dolphins make high-pitched sounds that **echo**, or bounce back, off objects. By listening to these echoes with their excellent hearing, bats can find insects to hunt. This method of locating food is called **echolocation**.

Symbiosis

Animals in **symbiotic relationships** help one another. Insects bite this hippopotamus, so it lets a bird land on its back to eat the insects. The hippo gets a cleaning, and the bird finds a meal!

Food for simple animals

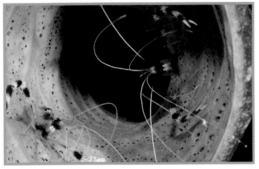

Sponges wait for food to come to them.

The sea anemone's tentacles contain stingers that paralyze small fish.

Simple animals have no head or brain, nor do they have a sense of smell, taste, sight, or hearing. Sponges, sea fans, sea anemones, and sea stars are simple animals. Even though they have no brain, their bodies are built to allow the animals to trap food.

I can't move!

Sponges live underwater. Their bodies are attached to rocks or hard surfaces so they cannot move. They eat by sucking in water and straining bits of food from it. Sea fans and sea anemones also live in one spot. These animals have only a stomach and stinging tentacles. They use their tentacles to trap and stun fish.

Five feet, one mouth

Sea stars hunt for food. They have small, hollow tube "feet" that act like suction cups, clinging onto prey such as shellfish. They use their "feet" to pry open their prey. This sea star has trapped a small fish.

Worms of all kinds

There are thousands of types of worms. Worms are **invertebrates**. Invertebrates are animals that have no spinal column. Most worms live underground, but some live underwater. Many worms, such as tapeworms, are **parasites**. They get nutrients from feeding off the bodies of **hosts**, or other animals.

Eat dirt!

As earthworms move underground, they make tunnels by swallowing soil. The soil passing through a worm's body is rich in nutrients, which the worm absorbs as food. The soil is then released by the worm and left behind in strings called **worm casts**. Worm casts and tunnels enrich the soil with nutrients and oxygen.

Wet worms

Worms that live underwater are called **marine** worms. Some marine worms have tiny bristly legs that allow them to move in water. Strong jaws help them eat small animals. Many marine worms are scavengers that help keep the seabed clean by eating dead creatures.

Feather duster worms stay anchored to one spot for their whole life. They wait for food to drift by and then grab it with their "feather-like" tentacles in the same way a feather duster grabs dust.

How do mollusks find a meal?

Clams, oysters, and scallops (shown above), have two shells that open and close for protection. They feed by drawing water inside their shell and straining tiny bits of plants and animals from the water.

Mollusks are animals such as slugs, snails, clams, and squid. Like worms, mollusks have a soft body and no skeleton. Some are herbivores, whereas others are hunters.

Snail's pace

Slugs and snails crawl along the ground and over plants, looking for food and eating as they go. Most snails and slugs eat plants, but some are carnivorous. They eat slow-moving prey such as earthworms and other slugs.

Quick and crafty

Octopuses, squid, and cuttlefish are powerful swimmers that can move quickly to escape danger or chase prey. Cuttlefish and octopuses use camouflage to hide while they wait for their prey. They can change the color of their body to blend in with their environment.

(left) The octopus has a round body and eight tentacles with suction cups that grab prey. This octopus uses its powerful jaws to crush a crab.

Crabby hunters and scavengers

An **arthropod** is an animal with a soft body covered in a hard **exoskeleton**. This animal group contains more kinds of animals than any other group and includes crabs, insects, and spiders.

Lobsters live on the ocean floor. They trap small animals with their sharp claws. Lobsters even eat other lobsters. They are fierce fighters that defend their home against enemies. The enemy often becomes the lobster's next meal!

Instead of hunting, some crabs wait for prey to wander within reach. Ghost crabs bury themselves in sand with only their eyes sticking out to spot prey. Crabs are also scavengers. They search the sand for bits of animals left behind by other hunters, such as pieces of fish dropped by gulls.

Crabs eat worms, snails, small fish, aquatic reptiles, and frogs. They grab animals with their strong claws.

Omnivorous insects

Insects have antennae for smelling plants. Some insects are attracted to plants of a certain color.

This pandora sphinx butterfly tastes with its feet.

Insects are arthropods with six legs. Fleas, ants, flies, butterflies, and bees are all insects, but they eat different things. Fleas are parasites that live off the blood of other animals. Plant-eating insects use their sensitive **antennae** to find plants. Antennae are thin, moveable sensory organs.

Feet feelers

Flies and butterflies use their feet to sense whether what they land on is food. These insects have special saliva that breaks down their food and **liquifies**, or turns it into juice. They then suck up the juice through their **proboscis**, or long tubular mouth part.

They eat *what*?!

The dung beetle, shown left, feeds on the droppings of other animals. It takes pieces of undigested fruits, seeds, and plants from these droppings, forms them into a ball, and rolls the ball away to bury it in a safe place. Not many animals eat dung, so there is always plenty of food for these beetles!

The praying mantis spends most of its time sitting motionless on branches or flowers. When a bee or other insect comes close enough, the mantis attacks quickly with its giant forelegs. Its forelegs snap shut like a nutcracker to catch and crush the insect.

Traps and poison

Like insects, spiders, inject saliva into their prey to liquefy the insides. They then suck up the liquid.

Arthropods with eight legs are called **arachnids**. This group includes mites, scorpions, spiders, and **harvestmen** (daddy longlegs). Most spiders use venom to kill or paralyze their prey. Spiders that feed on larger prey have more powerful poison. Spiders eat mainly insects such as bees, wasps, beetles, grasshoppers, and flies.

What a web they weave!

Some spiders build webs in which they trap their prey. These spiders have poor eyesight but an excellent sense of touch. A web-spinning spider waits until it feels something struggling in its sticky web. Once caught, the spider injects the prey with venom or wraps it in a sac to eat it later.

Gotcha!

Wandering spiders catch prey by **stalking** and **pouncing**. These spiders have good eyesight and are fierce hunters. Brazilian ant-eating spiders **mimic**, or look like, ants so they can crawl right into ant territory to hunt.

Blending in

Some spiders use camouflage to find food. These spiders hide easily because their bodies match their surroundings closely.

Instead of traveling to find food, spiders eat insects that wander near their hiding places. When the prey is within reach, the spider pounces and injects its victim with venom.

Trapping prey

Some animals set traps for their prey. The trapdoor spider lives in an underground silk-lined burrow covered by a silk lid. The spider waits behind the door until it feels the vibrations of prey passing by. It pops out to grab the prey.

trapdoor spider

Tarantula!

Tarantulas live in underground burrows and come out to hunt at night. They move slowly, so they usually sit still until prey approaches them. They eat insects, rodents, and small amphibians. Some South American tarantulas even eat small birds and rattlesnakes!

The name "tarantula" was first given to a species of wolf spider in Taranto, Italy. People believed that the spider's bite caused a victim to cry, run around, and dance uncontrollably. Now scientists know that tarantula bites are not very harmful to humans, even though they hurt a lot!

Fish food

Fish live in water. Some are herbivores that eat only plants. Other freshwater fish eat plants, but some also hunt for insects or smaller fish. Many fish eat **plankton**, which are tiny plants and animals that float in lakes and oceans.

Thousands of different types of fish live in the ocean. Some live in warm **tropical** waters. Others live in cold deep-sea waters. Sharks move around from place to place. Moray eels and manta rays are fish that live in or near the **coral reefs** of oceans.

The coral reef is full of places to hide and find food. Many fish find food in the holes and crevices.

Skilled hunters

All animals give off tiny amounts of electricity. Like other fish, sharks have a **lateral line** running down the sides of their bodies, which allows them to sense this electricity and find prey. Sharks also have an excellent sense of smell that helps them detect the scent of blood. Sharks can find fish hiding in murky waters or buried under sand.

lateral line

Camouflage

stingray

Many fish use camouflage to hide from prey. Stonefish have bodies that resemble stones or other natural objects. Underwater animals often climb over a stonefish without realizing it is a hungry predator! Fish such as flounders and stingrays have flat bodies. They bury themselves in the ocean floor, lie still, and wait for prey to come close. Stingrays also have a sharp poisonous spine in their tail with which they stun fish.

This frog fits a long worm into its huge mouth. It has no teeth, so it must swallow its prey whole.

Amphibian food

Frogs, toads, and salamanders are **amphibians**. Amphibians start their lives in water and can live both in water and on land. Most amphibians have a large mouth and no teeth. They swallow their food whole. All adult amphibians are carnivores. They eat any live animal they can swallow, including insects, spiders, snails, slugs, and earthworms. Large frogs eat mice, rats, small birds, and even small frogs.

A flick of the tongue

Frogs and toads have large appetites. They eat a lot of food! When they cannot find food, however, amphibians can go a long time before they must eat again.

Frogs and toads are good at catching flying insects. When they spot an insect, they flick out their sticky tongue, snatch the insect, and pull it into their mouth. Many frogs use their strong legs to leap out of water and catch passing insects in midair.

Reptilian hunters

Snakes, lizards, and turtles are **reptiles**. Reptiles come in several shapes and sizes, from the tiny gecko to the enormous Komodo dragon. Reptiles find food in a variety of ways. Some use poison, some choke their prey, and some devour rotting animals.

Built for hunting

Chameleons have several adaptations that help them find and catch food. They can change their appearance to blend in with their surroundings.

They sit still and move only their eyes to locate prey. When an insect comes close, the chameleon, shown above, shoots out its sticky tongue, grabs the insect, and pulls it into its mouth.

Snakes

All snakes are carnivorous. Small snakes eat small prey. Large snakes eat animals as big as antelopes. Boas **constrict**, or squeeze, their prey. They wrap their body around the prey and tighten their muscles until the prey stops breathing.

Snake sense

Snakes have sharp senses that alert them to nearby prey. A snake's body feels the vibrations made by animals as they move on the ground. **Heat-sensing pits** on a snake's face detect the body heat of other animals. Some snakes and lizards have a **Jacobson's organ** on the roof of their mouth that they use to identify scents.

What big teeth you have!

Poisonous snakes have sharp, hollow front teeth called **fangs**. Venom sacs in the snake's head release poison into the fangs. When a snake bites into its prey, the poison travels through the hollow fangs and into the wound. Some snake venom is strong enough to kill. Other snakes use venom to paralyze prey and then eat it alive while it cannot move.

Snakes do not chew their food—they swallow it whole. Hinges on their jaws allow them to open their mouth wide enough to swallow animals that are larger than themselves.

Lying in wait!

Crocodiles and alligators are patient hunters. They lie low in the water with only their eyes, ears, and nostrils above the surface. They wait for animals to come and drink at the water's edge and lunge from the water to grab their prey with their powerful jaws.

Making their meal last

When they detect prey, these huge reptiles flip or drag it underwater and drown it. They can run quickly on land to chase prey as well. Crocodiles and alligators often store food underwater. A crocodile can feed on a single antelope for many weeks!

The Komodo dragon

The Komodo dragon, shown top right, uses its keen senses of sight and smell to find food. Like a snake, it can unhinge its jaws to swallow large prey, sometimes in one gulp. It hunts and kills animals, but it also eats the rotting flesh of dead animals.

Big turtles

The green sea turtle finds its food underwater. Instead of legs, this turtle has flippers, which are much better for swimming. Unlike other turtles, green sea turtles travel great distances to feeding grounds, where they feast on fish. Sometimes they even eat birds!

It's all in the beak!

All birds have feathers, wings, a beak, and two legs. A bird's body is adapted to the type of food it eats. For example, some birds have strong beaks for breaking open nuts or seeds. Other birds have long, thin beaks for drinking nectar from flowers.

A yellow weaver uses its keen senses of sight and smell to catch an insect.

Chasing insects

Many birds eat insects. They have long, narrow beaks that work like tweezers to pluck insects from inside tree trunks or from the air. To catch prey, flycatchers are able to change direction quickly while flying.

Wading for food

Wading birds, such as avocets and herons, have long legs and long, thin beaks. Avocets use their bill to probe into sand or mud for shellfish and insect **larvae**. Herons stand quietly in deeper water, waiting to snap up a fish in their long bill.

Hummingbirds flap their wings very quickly in order to hover over flowers and suck out the nectar.

avocet

Birds of prey

Raptors such as eagles, hawks, and owls have strong, hooked beaks for tearing apart prey. These birds are carnivores. Their bodies are designed for hunting. Raptors have excellent eyesight that helps them spot prey from high in the air. Their sharp claws are perfect for grabbing prey as they swoop down.

(above) This osprey has caught a fish and found a high perch on which to enjoy its meal.

(right) Owls such as this barn owl swoop down from tall perches and catch mice or small birds. A barn-owl family can eat 6000 mice in a year!

Food for mammals

The first food for most mammals is milk from their mother. All female mammals have **mammary glands**, which make milk for their babies. Adult mammals have a variety of diets. Some eat plants, some eat animals, and some eat both.

Pandas are browsers. They prefer to eat specific types of bamboo shoots. When these plants are not available, pandas may starve.

Animals such as elephants, kangaroos, and zebras spend most of their time grazing on grass and tiny plants.

Browsers eat mainly the leaves of plants. Giraffes, antelope, and deer are browsers.

Carnivores and omnivores

Most carnivores and omnivores have sharp teeth or claws and strong jaws to grab and tear apart food. Speed is also important for animals when trying to catch prey. Lions, tigers, bobcats, cheetahs, and cougars are all cats that use strength, speed, and cunning. They chase down their prey and pounce on it to bring it down. Lions and other meat-eaters, such as wolves, cooperate when they hunt.

(top right) Some predators pounce on their prey. (center) Predators attack weak or old animals in a herd and keep herds healthy as a result. (below) Large cats such as tigers and lions have sharp canine teeth for piercing flesh.

(right) Omnivores such as raccoons and some bears eat almost anything they can find.

Using echolocation to find food

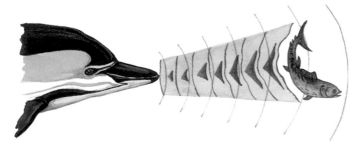

Dolphins and bats use echolocation to locate food. Instead of using their eyes, they use echoes to find objects. These animals make high-pitched sounds that bounce off objects in their path, creating echoes. The animal senses the echoes and can tell whether the object ahead is food. It can even tell which kind of food it is.

A stunning song

Humpback whales, shown below, hunt together in a **pod**. The lead whale sings a song that frightens schools of fish into a tight group. The whales then lunge through the water and catch mouthfuls of fish. Each whale plays a role in this method of **cooperative hunting**.

Where are my tools?

A few animals use tools to find food or to break it open. Sea otters use rocks to pry shellfish off the ocean floor and to break the shells. Chimpanzees use stones to crack nuts. They also use sticks as tools. A chimp pokes a twig into an insect nest, termite mound, or into the ground. When it pulls out the stick, there are insects clinging to it. The chimp eats them and tries again!

This chimpanzee is using a stick to "fish" for food in a termite mound.

(below) The black-breasted buzzard likes to eat emu eggs, but the eggs are too big to lift. To open the eggs, the buzzard smashes them with a stone.

How humans find food

Humans eat many kinds of foods to get the nutrients they need. Many are omnivores.

Humans are also part of the animal kingdom. We eat fruit, vegetables, dairy products, and meat. Some humans are **vegetarians**, who do not eat meat. Instead of finding their own food, most people rely on farmers to grow fruits and vegetables and raise animals. People then buy these foods in supermarkets. Many people, however, do not have enough to eat. You can help fight hunger by donating to a local food bank or supporting organizations such as UNICEF that help feed people. You can also visit www.thehungersite.com.

Unlike animals, humans have learned how to grow and raise food and always know where to find it! Farmers grow fruits and vegetables and raise animals for dairy and meat. We buy the food in stores.

Competing for food

Humans can live in different places, but most other animals cannot. When people clear land to build houses, the animals that live there lose their homes. Without a place to live, eat, and raise young, animals cannot survive.

Tropical rain forests are disappearing because huge areas of trees are cut down and burned to make room for farmland. Each year thousands of species of animals and plants become **endangered** or **extinct**. Every year in Africa, thousands of wilderness acres are taken over to build cities and farms. Losing wilderness areas threatens the lives of animals such as elephants and cheetahs, which need large areas to roam and find food.

Finding food near people

Many animals have better luck finding food in human habitats than in their own habitats. Deer and elk often find food in towns and cities. Bears, rats, and raccoons find food in garbage cans. Foxes and coyotes prey on domestic animals. Farms attract insects, rodents, and many other animals. Even large animals, such as elephants and cougars, will visit farms to look for food they cannot find anywhere else.

More and more, humans and other animals must compete for food! Wildlife organizations such as the World Wildlife Fund can tell you how you can help save animal habitats.

Words to know

adapt To become different to suit a new habitat

antennae A pair of flexible feelers on the head of an invertebrate such as an insect

camouflage A color pattern on an animal that allows it to hide from enemies

cooperative feeding Working together in a group to catch food

coral reef An area of the ocean made up of living coral and skeletons of dead coral

ecosystem A community of living things that are connected to one another and to the surroundings in which they live

endangered Describing a living thing that is in danger of becoming extinct

energy The physical power needed for moving and breathing

exoskeleton A hard shell that covers the outside of an invertebrate's body and protects it

extinct Describing a plant or animal that no longer exists

host The animal or plant on which a parasite lives

invertebrate An animal without a backbone

Jacobson's organ An organ used for taste and smell found on the roof of the mouth of some reptiles

lateral line A line of pores along both sides of the body of a fish used for sensing differences in water pressure and depth

mammary gland An organ in a female mammal that produces milk for her young

marine Describing animals that live in the sea

mimic To look like something else

nutrient Ingredients in food that promote healthy growth and development

parasites Tiny insects or animals that live on the bodies of other animals or plants

pod A group of marine mammals such as whales

reptile A cold-blooded vertebrate covered with scales or horny plates

stalk To track prey quietly and carefully

symbiotic relationship A close relationship between two or more organisms of different species for the benefit of both

tropical Describing hot, wet climate

venomous Describing animals that produce poison

Index

1 2 3 4 5 6 7 8 9 0   Printed in the U.S.A.   0 9 8 7 6 5 4 3 2 1